I SING FOR JOY

I Sing for Joy

MUSIC FROM THE RTÉ RADIO ONE
CHURCH MUSIC COMPETITIONS

Edited by
Paul Kenny
in association with
Mary Curtin

the columba press

First published in 2006 by
the columba press
55A Spruce Avenue, Stillorgan Industrial Park, Blackrock, Co Dublin

Cover by Bill Bolger
Music setting by Matthew Hébert
Printed in Ireland by
ColourBooks Ltd, Dublin

ISBN 1-85607-370-X

Table of Contents

Hymns

Psalms

Anthems and Motets

Preface

As part of our continuing commitment to Public Service Broadcasting, and in particular to Religious broadcasting, RTÉ Radio 1 has organised two competitions (in 1997 and 2001) for liturgical music suitable for use in regular Sunday worship.

The purpose of these competitions was two-fold: firstly to encourage Irish composers of liturgical music, who would otherwise have few opportunities to publicise their work and, secondly, to provide new, Irish-composed music which would be suitable for use by ordinary parish choirs. Our experience of broadcasting two Sunday liturgies every week, since the inception of RTÉ Radio 80 years ago, had shown us that there was a heavy reliance on international sources for music in weekly liturgies. Yet we also believed that there were many Irish composers with an interest in this genre of music.

I am happy to say that our confidence was well-founded. RTÉ was delighted with the level of interest shown in the competitions and the adjudicators, both national and international, were very impressed with the quality of the entries. They confirmed that the winning pieces were up to the highest international standard and they congratulated RTÉ Radio 1 for organising 'a unique project by a Public Sector Broadcaster'.

I am delighted that The Columba Press has decided to publish a selection of the music from the finals of both competitions. The pieces in this book have also been recorded by Radio 1 and are available on a CD of the same name (*I Sing For Joy*). Together, the book and CD will provide a valuable resource for both choirs and liturgists and, I hope, will enable Irish-composed liturgical music to receive the recognition and popularity it so richly deserves.

Adrian Moynes
Managing Director, RTÉ Radio

Mass of Thanksgiving
KYRIE

Sue Furlong

Ky - ri - e   e - le - i - son.

Cantor + Congregation (+ Sopranos)

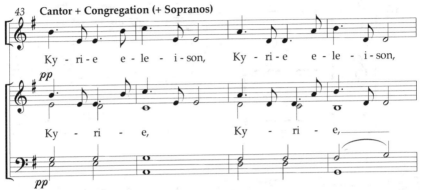

Ky - ri - e   e - le - i - son,   Ky - ri - e   e - le - i - son,

Ky - ri - e,   Ky - ri - e,_____

molto rall.

Ky - ri - e   e - le - i - son.

Ky - ri - e   e - lei - son.
Ky - ri - e_____ e - lei - son.

Ky - ri - e   e - lei - son.

Mass of Thanksgiving

GLORIA

Sue Furlong

REFRAIN (Congregation sing the melody)

14

peace to his peo - ple, his peo - ple on earth.____

peace to his peo - ple, his peo - ple on earth.____

For

Glo - ry to God in the high - est.

you a-lone are the Ho-ly One, you a-lone are the Lord,

You____ a - lone, you are the Lord,

You a-lone are the Most High, Je - sus Christ,____ with the

Ho - ly Spi - rit, in the glo - ry of God the Fa - ther.

REFRAIN Glo - ry to God in the high - est!

Glo - ry to God! Glo - ry to God!

Glo - ry to God in the high - est, and

Glo - ry to God! Glo - ry to God, and

peace to his peo - ple, his peo - ple on earth.____

peace to his peo - ple, his peo - ple on earth.____

Glo - ry to God in the high - est.

ff

A-men.__ A - men!__ A - men!__ A - men!__

ff

molto rall. *ff*

A - men,__ A - men!

ff

Mass of Thanksgiving
ALLELUIA

Be filled with joy as you sing!

Sue Furlong

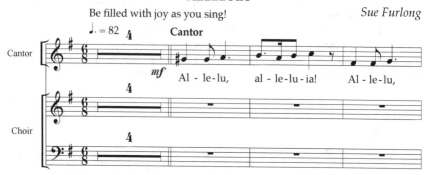

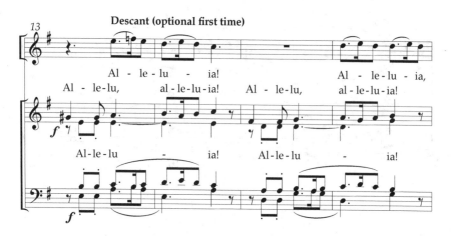

Al-le-lu-ia! Al - le-lu - ia!
Al - le-lu - ia, al-le-lu-ia! Al-le-lu - ia!

Al - le-lu - ia, al-le-lu-ia! Al-le-lu - ia!

Open our hearts, O Lord, to accept the words of your Son.

Descant

Al - le-lu - ia! Al - le-lu - ia,
Al - le-lu, al-le-lu-ia! Al - le-lu, al-le-lu-ia!

Al-le-lu - ia! Al-le-lu - ia!

rall.

Al-le-lu-ia! Al - le-lu - ia!
Al - le-lu - ia, al-le-lu-ia! Al-le-lu - ia!

Al - le-lu - ia, al-le-lu-ia! Al-le-lu - ia!

19

Mass of Thanksgiving
SANCTUS

Sue Furlong

Mass of Thanksgiving
MEMORIAL ACCLAMATION

Sue Furlong

Mass of Thanksgiving
DOXOLOGY AND GREAT AMEN

Sue Furlong

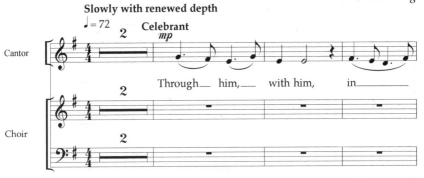

Through him, with him, in

him, in the un-i-ty of the Ho-ly Spi-rit,

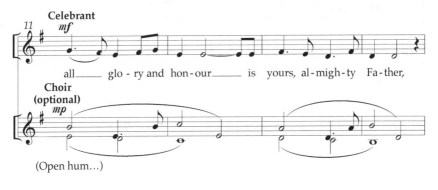

all glo-ry and hon-our is yours, al-migh-ty Fa-ther,

(Open hum...)

for ev-er and ev - er.

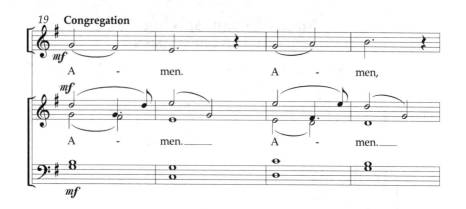

Mass of Thanksgiving
LAMB OF GOD

Sue Furlong

mer - cy on us. Lamb of God,

poco rall. Have mer - cy. Lamb of God,

you___ take a - way the sins of the world: grant us___ peace,

you___ take a - way the sins of the world:

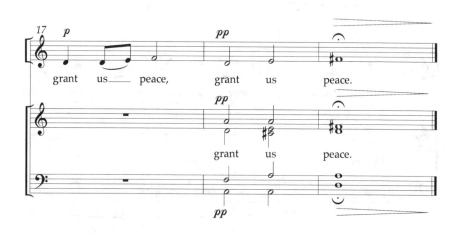

grant us___ peace, grant us peace.

grant us peace.

Mass of Thanksgiving
DISMISSAL

Sue Furlong

A Celtic Mass

KYRIE

Bernard Sexton

You_ plead for us at the right hand of the Fa - ther: Lord,_ have mer - cy.

Christ,_ have mer - cy.

Christ, have mer - cy.

Lord,_ have mer - cy.

Lord,_ have mer - cy.

A Celtic Mass
GLORIA

Bernard Sexton

worship you, we give you thanks, we praise you for your

Glory to God in the highest,
glory! Glory to God in the highest, and

peace to his people, his people on earth. Glory to God in the
Glory to God in the highest,

high est, and peace to his people, his people on earth.

Lord Jesus Christ, only Son of the Father, Lord God, Lamb of

31

God. You take a-way the sin— of the world: have

mer - cy— on us. You are seat-ed at the right hand of the

Fa - ther: re - ceive_____ our prayer.

Glo - ry to God in the high-est, ___

Glo - ry to God in the high - est and peace to his peo-ple, his

Glo - ry to God in the high-est, ___

peo - ple on earth. ___ Glo - ry to God in the high - est, and

Glo - ry to God in the high - est,____

peo - ple on earth.____ Glo - ry to God in the high - est, and

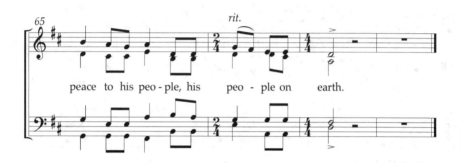

rit.

peace to his peo - ple, his   peo - ple on   earth.

A Celtic Mass
ALLELUIA

Bernard Sexton

A Celtic Mass

LENTEN
GOSPEL ACCLAMATION

Bernard Sexton

A Celtic Mass
EUCHARISTIC ACCLAMATIONS

Bernard Sexton

Sanctus

Memorial Acclamation

Dy-ing you de-stroyed our death, ris-ing you re-stored our life. Lord Je-sus come in glo - ry! come.

Dy - ing, dy - ing, ris - ing, ris - ing, come in glo - ry, Lord Je - sus, come!

Come! Come!

Great Amen

A Celtic Mass
AGNUS DEI

Bernard Sexton

A Celtic Mass
DISMISSAL

Bernard Sexton

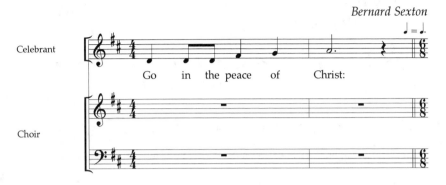

Celebrant

Go in the peace of Christ:

Choir

With Energy

Thanks, thanks be to God!

Eucharistic Acclamations

Holy, Holy

John McCann

Memorial Acclamation

Christ has— died, Christ is— ri-sen, Christ will— come a - gain.

The Doxology uses the formula given in the Missal, which depending on the voice of the Presider begins

either:

Through him...   or: Through him...

Great Amen

A - men, A - men, A - men,— A - men.

Festive Gloria

John McCann

Fa - ther:_____ re-ceive__ our prayer.

mf

right hand of the Fa - ther: re-ceive__ our prayer.

Fa - ther:_____ *mf* re-ceive our prayer.

Cantor/Choir
mf

Glo - ry to God in the high - est and

Descant (optional)
f

Glo -

All *f*

peace to God's peo - ple on earth. Glo - ry to God in the

ry, glo - ry to God!

Cantor/Choir
mf

high - est and peace to God's peo - ple on earth. For

you a - lone are the Ho - ly One, you a - lone are__ the Lord,

divisi

cresc.

you a - lone are the Most High, Je - sus Christ,_____ with the Ho - ly

48

Mass of Christ the King
PENITENTIAL RITE

John McCann

Mass of St. Mark
GLORIA

Ephrem Feeley

Choir

we wor-ship you,___ we give you thanks,___ we

praise you for___ your glo - ry.

Congregation

Glo-ry to God in the high-est hea-vens, glo-ry to God__ and

peace on earth. Glo-ry to God in the high-est hea-vens,

peace to all on earth!

Cantor

Lord Je - sus Christ,

on - ly Son of the Fa - ther, Lord__ God,

Lamb of God, you take a-way the sin of the world: have

mer - cy on us, have mer - cy on us. You are seat-ed at the right hand,___ at the right hand of the Fa-ther: re - ceive___ our___ prayer, re - ceive our prayer. Glo-ry to God in the high-est hea-vens, glo-ry to God___ and peace on earth.___ Glo-ry to God in the

high-est hea-vens, peace to all on earth!

Choir *unison*
marcato

For you a-lone are the Ho-ly One,

divisi

you a-lone are the Lord. You a-lone are the

subito **p**

Most High, Je-sus Christ. With the Ho - ly

subito **p**

cresc.

Spi - rit, in the glo - ry of God the Fa - ther, A -

cresc.

A - men, A - men, A - men!

men,

A - men, A - men, A - men!

Mass in Honour of Mary
GLORIA

Ger Lawlor

Mass of St. Finbarr
GLORIA

Patrick Killeen

Refrain

Cantor / Choir: Glo - ri - a, glo - ri - a in ex - cel - sis De - o, glo - ri - a, glo - ri - a in ex - cel - sis De - o, glo - ri - a, glo - ri - a in ex - cel - sis De - o.

1. Glo - ry to God in the high - est and peace to his peo - ple on earth. Lord God, hea - ven - ly King, al - migh - ty God and Fa - ther, we wor - ship you, we give you thanks, we praise you for your glo - ry.

To Refrain

2. Lord Je - sus Christ, on - ly Son of the Fa - ther,
Lord God, Lamb of God, you who take a -
way the sin of the world: have mer - cy on us.

To Refrain

3. You are seat-ed at the right hand of the Fa - ther: re -
ceive our prayer. For you a - lone are the Ho - ly One. For
you a-lone are the Lord. For you a-lone are the Most High, Je - sus
Christ, with the Ho - ly Spi - rit, in the

To Final Refrain

glo - ry of God the Fa - ther.

61

Final Refrain

Glo - ri - a, glo - ri - a in ex - cel - sis De - o, glo - ri - a, glo - ri - a

in ex - cel - sis De - o, glo - ri - a, glo - ri - a in ex - cel - sis De - o.

Mass of St. Richard

EUCHARISTIC ACCLAMATIONS

Andrew Johnstone

Memorial Acclamation No. 1

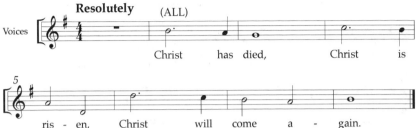

Christ has died, Christ is ris - en, Christ will come a - gain.

Memorial Acclamation No. 2

Dy-ing you de - stroyed our death, ris - ing you re-stored our life. Lord Je-sus, come in glo - ry.

Memorial Acclamation No. 3

When we eat this bread and drink this cup, we pro - claim your death Lord Je - sus, un - til you come in glo - ry.

Memorial Acclamation No. 4

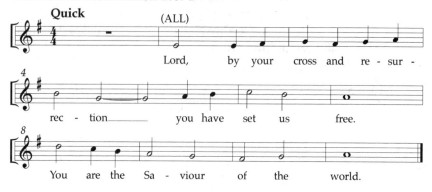

Quick

(ALL)

Lord, by your cross and re - sur - rec - tion you have set us free. You are the Sa - viour of the world.

Great Amen No. 1

Majestically

(ALL)

A - men.

Great Amen No. 2

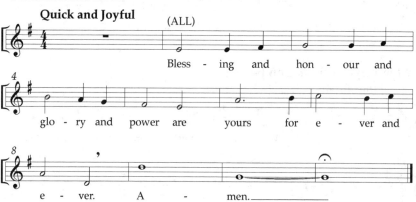

Quick and Joyful

(ALL)

Bless - ing and hon - our and glo - ry and power are yours for e - ver and e - ver. A - men.

Ár nAthair

Sean P. McKiernan

Ár__ n–Ath-air 'tá'r neamh, go__ nao - far_____

dA-inm, go dta-ga do ríocht, go ndéan-tar do thoil ar a'

tal-amh mar a ní-thear ar neamh. Ár n–a-rán lae-

thiú - il, tabhair dúinn in - niu, a-gus

maith__ dúinn ár bfhia - cha, mar mhaith-i-mid dár

bhféi-chiú-na féin._____ Is ná lig__ sinn i

gca - thú, ach__ saor sinn, saor sinn ó olc.

Mass for the Body of Christ
FRACTION RITE:
LAMB OF GOD / WE ARE ONE BODY

Ian Callanan

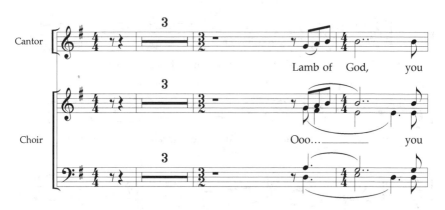

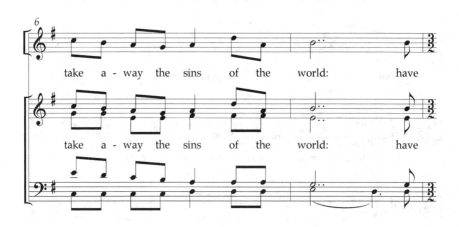

Repeat 3 times

mer - cy on us.   Bread__ of life,   you
                   Wine__ of peace,_____
                   Son__ of God,_____

Repeat 3 times

mer - cy on us.   O Lamb of God,

Ooo..._____ you

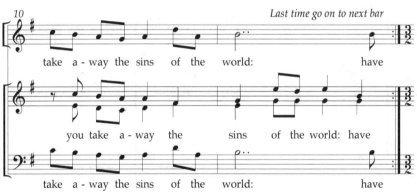

Last time go on to next bar

take a - way the sins of the world: have

you take a - way the sins of the world: have

take a - way the sins of the world: have

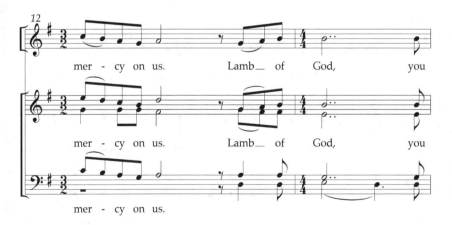

mer - cy on us.   Lamb__ of God,   you

mer - cy on us.   Lamb__ of God,   you

mer - cy on us.

take a-way the sins of the world: grant us___ peace.

End here if not using hymn

take a-way the sins of the world: grant us___ peace

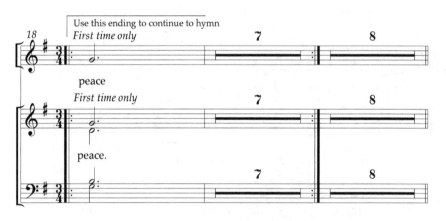

Use this ending to continue to hymn

First time only

7   8

peace

First time only

7   8

peace.

7   8

Refrain

We are one bread, we are one bo-dy, gath-ered as

We are one bread, we are one bo-dy, gath-ered as

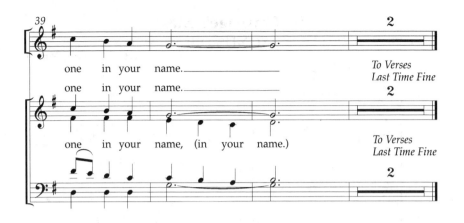

one   in your   name._____

To Verses
Last Time Fine

one   in your   name._____

one   in your   name, (in your name.)

To Verses
Last Time Fine

Verses

1. All   who hun - ger, gath - er glad - ly, Je - sus is   our
2. You who thirst for days of full - ness shall be wel - comed
3. Taste and see that God is good,____ Je - sus, liv - ing
4. In   this feast we taste your good - ness, bread and wine of

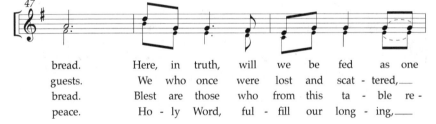

bread.   Here,   in   truth, will we be fed as one
guests.   We who once were lost and scat - tered,____
bread.   Blest are those who from this ta - ble re -
peace.   Ho - ly Word, ful - fill our long - ing,____

To Refrain

bo - dy   in   Christ._____
ne - ver thirst a - gain._____
ceive and live in   truth._____
fill us with your grace._____

St. Carthage's Mass
AGNUS DEI

Jan van Putten

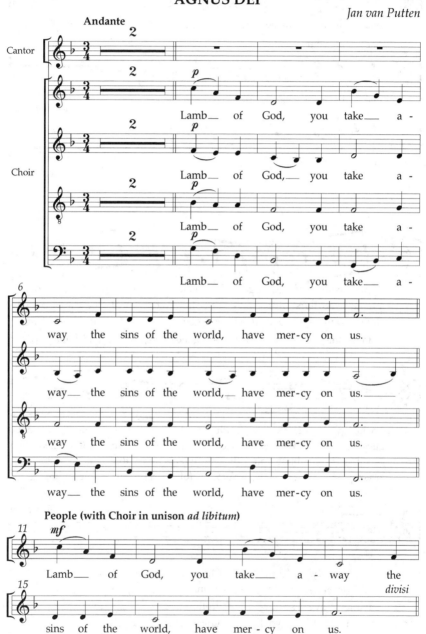

70

Holy Spirit, Lord of Light

Pentecost Sequence

John McCann

1. Ho ly Spi - rit Lord of light, From the clear ce -
2. Thou, of all con - sol - ers best, Thou, the soul's de -
3. Light im - mor - tal light di - vine, Vis - it thou these
4. Heal our wounds, our strength re - new; On our dry - ness
5. Thou, on us who e - ver more, Thee con - fess and

(1) les - tial height, Thy pure beam - ing ra - diance give.
(2) light - ful guest, Dost re - fresh - ing peace_ be - stow;
(3) hearts of thine, And our in - most be - ing fill:
(4) pour_ thy dew; Wash the stains of guilt_ a - way;
(5) thee_ a - dore, with thy sev'n - fold gifts_ de - scend:

(1) Come thou Fa - ther of_ the poor, come with trea - sures
(2) Thou in toil are com - fort sweet; Plea - sant cool - ness
(3) If thou take thy grace_ a - way, No - thing pure in
(4) Bend the stub - born heart_ and will; melt the froz - en,
(5) Give us com - fort when_ we die; Give us life with

(1) which_ en - dure; Come, thou light____ of all__ that live.
(2) in____ the heat, So - lace in____ the midst_ of woe.
(3) us____ will stay; All our good____ is turned to ill.
(4) warm_ the chill; Guide the steps____ that go_ a - stray.
(5) thee_ on high; Give us joys____ that ne - ver end.

Bua An Uain

Peadar Breslin

1. A Íosa, Uain Dé,___ déin tró - cai - re or - ainn! A
2. A Íosa, Uain Dé,___ maith dúinn___ ár bpeach - aí! A
3. A Íosa, Uain Dé,___ tabhair dúinn___ do ghrá - sta! A

Íosa, Uain Dé,___ déin tró - cai - re! Ag an
Íosa, Uain Dé,___ maith dúinn___ ár n–olc! Ar an
Íosa, Uain Dé,___ tabhair dúinn___ do ghrá! Cé gur

m–bord roimh do pháis,___ d'fhág tú cómhar-tha ded' ghrá___ 'san a–
gcrois gharbh - ua - far, bhí do chroí lán de ghrá,___ dod'
géar bhí do chéas-adh, is do luath - chur gan grad-am, Ba

ránn is an fhíon ós do chómhair.___ Ach i
mhuin - tir, a ghabh thart gan suim;___ Do
ghlór - mhar do bhua ar an mbás;___ Dé

measc do lucht to - fa, bhí an duin - e a bhraith thú. A
mháth - air, chroí - bhris - te, do dheas - cab - ail scaip - the, A
hAoi - ne do - bhrón - ach, ach Domh-nach geal ór - ga, A

Íosa, Uain Dé,___ déin tró - cai - re!
Íosa, Uain Dé,___ maith dúinn___ ár n–olc!
Íosa, Uain Dé,___ tabhair dúinn___ do ghlóir!

Bua An Uain - The Victory Of The Lamb

Peadar Breslin

As We Walked Home At Close Of Day

John L. Bell & Graham Maule   *Rachel F. Pike*

1. As___ we walked home at close of day, a___
2. 'Why wan - der fur - ther with - out light? Please
3. We___ sat to eat our sim - ple spread, then___
4. No___ stran - ger he; it was our eyes which
5. Al - le - lu - ia, al - le - lu - ia! Al -

(1) stran - ger___ joined___ us___ on our way. He___
(2) stay___ with___ us___ this___ troub - led night. We've___
(3) watched the___ stran - ger___ take the bread; and,___
(4) failed___ to___ see___ in___ stran - ger's guise, the___
(5) le - lu - ia,___ al - le - lu - ia! As___

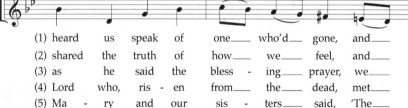

(1) heard us speak of one___ who'd___ gone, and___
(2) shared the truth of how___ we___ feel, and___
(3) as he said the bless - ing___ prayer, we___
(4) Lord who, ris - en from___ the___ dead, met___
(5) Ma - ry and our sis - ters___ said, 'The___

(1) when we stopped, he___ car - ried on.
(2) now would like to___ share a meal.'
(3) knew that some - one___ else was there.
(4) us when rea - dy___ to be fed.
(5) Lord is ris en___ from the dead!'

SATB Version

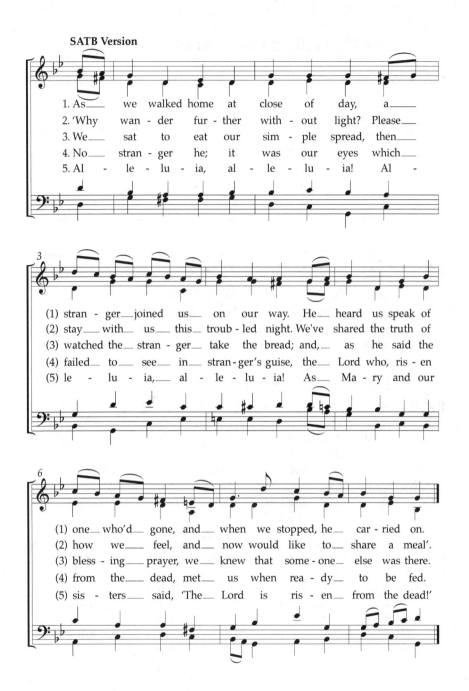

1. As we walked home at close of day, a
2. 'Why wan - der fur - ther with - out light? Please
3. We sat to eat our sim - ple spread, then
4. No stran - ger he; it was our eyes which
5. Al - le - lu - ia, al - le - lu - ia! Al -

(1) stran - ger joined us on our way. He heard us speak of
(2) stay with us this troub - led night. We've shared the truth of
(3) watched the stran - ger take the bread; and, as he said the
(4) failed to see in stran - ger's guise, the Lord who, ris - en
(5) le - lu - ia, al - le - lu - ia! As Ma - ry and our

(1) one who'd gone, and when we stopped, he car - ried on.
(2) how we feel, and now would like to share a meal'.
(3) bless - ing prayer, we knew that some - one else was there.
(4) from the dead, met us when rea - dy to be fed.
(5) sis - ters said, 'The Lord is ris - en from the dead!'

How Bright Those Glorious Spirits Shine
(Bright Spirits)

Isaac Watts (1674-1748)
and others

Kenneth Maybury

Maestoso

Voice

1. How bright those glori - ous (1) spi - rits shine! Whence all their white ar - (1) ray? How came they to the bliss - ful (1) seats of ev - er - last - ing day?

2. Lo! These are they, from (2) suff'r - ings great, who came to realms of (2) light, And in the Blood of Christ__ have (2) washed Those robes__ which shine so bright.

3. Now with tri - umph - al (3) palms they stand Be - fore the throne on (3) high, And serve the God they love,__ a - (3) midst The glo - ries of the sky.

4. Hun - ger and thirst are (4) felt no more, Nor suns with scorch - ing (4) ray; God is their sun, whose cheer - ing (4) beams Dif - fuse__ e - ter - nal day.

5. The Lamb, which dwells a - (5) midst the throne, Shall o'er them still pre - (5) side; Feed them with nour - ish - ment__ di - (5) vine, And all__ their foot - steps guide.

6. 'Mid pas - tures green he'll (6) lead his flock, Where liv - ing streams ap - (6) pear; And God, the Lord, from ev - 'ry (6) eye Shall wipe__ off ev - 'ry tear.

The Lord Our God Is Wonderful (Clonbroney)

Kenneth Maybury

1. The Lord our God is won - der - ful, And guides us as we go through life, and all its hap - pi - ness as well as some - times woe. He watch - es o - ver all of us and keeps us safe from harm. And sends His Ho - ly Spi - rit down with such be - guil - ing charm.

2. When on the road of life we pass through sick - ness, grief and strife, we must hold fast to Je - sus Christ, and let Him guide our life. He al - ways an - swers all our prayers and helps us on our way. And gives us hope to live that life that is the per - fect way.

We Sing Our Praise to You, Lord Jesus
(Abberley)

L. Ruth Hockey, (b. 1965)   *Kenneth Maybury*

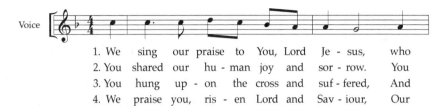

1. We sing our praise to You, Lord Je - sus, who
2. You shared our hu - man joy and sor - row. You
3. You hung up - on the cross and suf - fered, And
4. We praise you, ris - en Lord and Sav - iour, Our

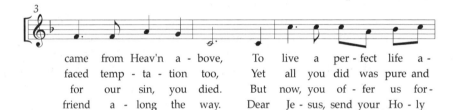

came from Heav'n a - bove, To live a per - fect life a -
faced temp - ta - tion too, Yet all you did was pure and
for our sin, you died. But now, you of - fer us for -
friend a - long the way. Dear Je - sus, send your Ho - ly

mong us, And show us God's great love.
ho - ly, And all your words were true.
give - ness, And call us to your side.
Spi - rit, And live in us to - day.

We Thank You, O Father (Zion)

L. Ruth Hockey (b. 1965)   *Kenneth Maybury*

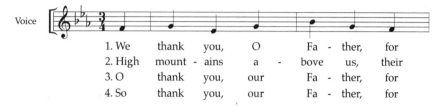

1. We thank you, O Father, for
2. High mount - ains a - bove us, their
3. O thank you, our Fa - ther, for
4. So thank you, our Fa - ther, for

all you have done, For mak - ing the
peaks capped with snow; Green grass on the
all in this life, For sis - ter and
send - ing your Son To help us and

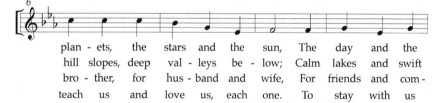

plan - ets, the stars and the sun, The day and the
hill slopes, deep val - leys be - low; Calm lakes and swift
bro - ther, for hus - band and wife, For friends and com -
teach us and love us, each one. To stay with us

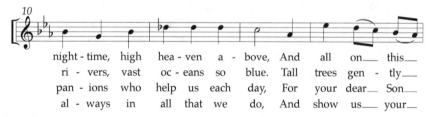

night - time, high hea - ven a - bove, And all on__ this__
ri - vers, vast oc - eans so blue. Tall trees gen - tly__
pan - ions who help us each day, For your dear__ Son__
al - ways in all that we do, And show us__ your__

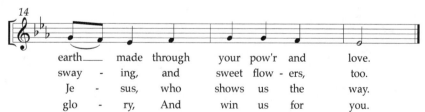

earth__ made through your pow'r and love.
sway - ing, and sweet flow - ers, too.
Je - sus, who shows us the way.
glo - ry, And win us for you.

80

Shepherd Song

Based on Psalm 23

Bernard Sexton

1. The___ Lord will be my shep - herd, there is
(2. As a) shep-herd knows the right___ path, so he
(3. Sure -ly) good-ness, sure - ly kind - ness shall___

no - thing I shall need. When I hun - ger, tired and
puts me on the way. On the straight road safe and
ev - er fol-low me. God, Pro - vi - der, God, Pro -

wea - ry, to green pas - tures me he leads; when my
care - less, nev - er chance that I will stray. Should I
tect - or, shall___ al - ways pres - ent be. In his

spi - rits fail he brings___ me to the wa - ters fresh and
walk in fields of dark - ness, no___ ev - il would I
house I'll dwell for - ev - er, at his right hand I will

calm, lov-ing shep-herd, gen - tle mas - ter, car-ing ten - der of this
fear, with the crook and staff he com - forts, and his pres-ence al-ways
stand. Nev-er strang-er, al-ways wel - comed by his lov-ing, car-ing

lamb.
near.
hand.

1, 2
2. As
3. Sure -

SATB arrangement

1. The____ Lord will be my shep - herd, there is no - thing I shall
2. As a shep - herd knows the right____ path, so he puts me on the
3. Sure - ly good - ness, sure - ly kind - ness shall____ e - ver fol - low

need. When I hun - ger, tired and wea - ry, to green
way, On the straight road, safe and care - less ne - ver
me. God, Pro - vi - der, God, Pro - tec - tor, shall____

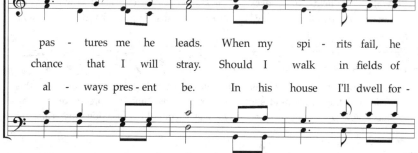

pas - tures me he leads. When my spi - rits fail, he
chance that I will stray. Should I walk in fields of
al - ways pres - ent be. In his house I'll dwell for -

brings__ me to the wa - ters fresh and calm;__ lov - ing
dark - ness, no__ e - vil would I fear,__ with the
e - ver, at his right hand I will stand.__ Nev - er

shep - herd, gen - tle Mas - ter, car - ing ten - der of this lamb.
crook and staff he com - forts and his pres - ence al - ways near.
strang - er, al - ways wel - comed by his lov - ing, car - ing hand.

Do Not Let Your Hearts Be Troubled

based on John 14: 1-7; 16:22;   *Patrick Killeen*

18 *unison*
Do not let your hearts be troub-led,___ trust in God and trust in

21
me; There are ma-ny rooms in my Fa-ther's House, if there

24 Men (*unison*)
were not I should have told you. I shall re-turn to take you with me

28
so that where I am, you may be too. I am the Way, the

31
Truth and the Life, if you know me you know my Fa-ther.

34
I will re-turn to take you with me. On that day you will

37 *unison*
cry with joy. Do not let your hearts be troub-led,___

40
trust in God and trust in me; There are ma-ny rooms in my

43
Fa-ther's House, if there were not I should have told you.

Taste And See That The Lord Is Good.

John Gibson
www.johncgibson.com
e-mail: johnnyg51@eircom.net

Refrain

Choir

Taste and see that the Lord is

To Verses

good;___ Blest are they who hope in God___

Verses

1. I   will   bless   the   Lord___   at   all
2. Glo - ri - fy   the   Lord___   with___
3. Look towards   God___   and   be   ra - di -

times, God's___ praise___ al - ways on my lips.___ In the
me,___ ⁊ To - geth - er let us praise God's name.___ I___
ant,___ Let your fac - es not___ be a - bashed, This___

Lord my soul shall make___ its boast;___ the
sought the Lord and he ans - wered me,___ from
poor man called, the Lord___ heard him and

To Refrain
Last time To Final Refrain

hum - ble shall praise God's name.___
all my ter - rors he___ set me free.
res - cued him from all___ his dis - tress.

Final Refrain

Taste and see that the Lord is good;— Blest are

they who hope in God____

Taispeáin Dúinn Slí na Beatha, A Thiarna

Salm 15

Michael Weedle

Freagra

Tais - peáin dúinn— slí na bea - tha, a Thiar - na.

Véarsaí

Caomhnaigh mé a Thiarna, is ortsa	a	thriallaim.
Beannaím an Tiarna as ucht comhairle	a	thabhairt dom,
Tá gairdeas ar mo chroí agus áthas	ar	m'anam,

Dearim leis an Tiarna: "Is	tú	mo	Dhi - a.
agus teagasc a thabhairt do mo	chroí	san	oi - che.
agus mairfidh mo cholainn faoi	shuaimh - neas	freis - in.

Is é an Tiarna is rogha liom: mo	chuid	de	réir oidhreachta.
Coimeádaim an Tiarna de	shíor	os	mo choinne:
Óir ní fhágfaidh tú m'anam	i	measc	na marbh,

agus cuid mo chailíse; is ort a -	tá	mo—	sheasamh!"
agus é ar mo dheasláimh ní chor -	ró	far mé	choíche.
ná ní ligfidh tú do do mhuirneach	trúail - liú	a	fheiceáil.

Lord, You Are My Shepherd

Psalm 23

Ephrem Feeley

Verse 2

Cantor

2. Lord, you guide me a - long the right path, you are

Choir

Lord you guide me in

true to your name.— If I should walk in the val-ley of death, no

paths that are right. I fear no - thing with

e - vil would I fear;— you are there with your crook and your staff,— with

you at my side. You are there,

rit. *To Main Response*

these you give me com - fort.

rit.

you are al - ways there.

Verse 3

Choir *unison*

slightly faster

3. You have pre - pared___ a ban-quet for me in the sight of my

divisi

foes.___ My head you have___ an - oint - ed with oil,___ my

rit. To Main Response

cup is ov - er - flow - ing.

Verse 4

Choir *unison*

slightly faster

4. Good - ness and kind - ness shall sure - ly fol - low me,

Descant

All the days of my life,___ I make my home___ in the

Choir

all the days of my life.___ I make my home___ in the

To Final Response

rit.

house of the Lord,___ and live with God for - ev - er.

divisi

rit.

house of the Lord,___ and live with God for - ev - er.

Final Response

Descant — a tempo

Lord, you are my shep - herd; in you __ I lack __ no - thing. __

Congregation — a tempo

Lord, you __ are my shep - herd; __ in you __ I lack no - thing. __

The Lord Is My Shepherd

Based on Psalm 23

Moira Gray

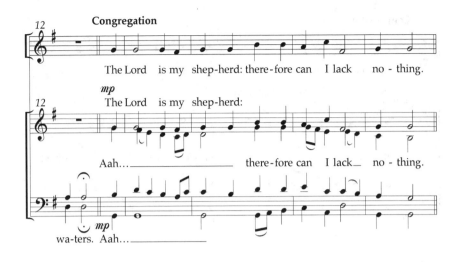

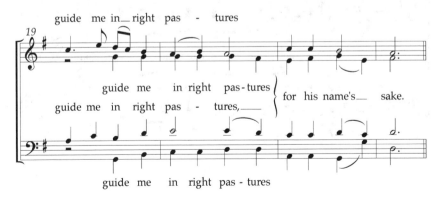

Congregation

The Lord is my shep-herd: there-fore can I lack no-thing.

The Lord is my shep-herd:

Aah... there-fore can I lack no-thing.

Aah...

Verse 3

a little slower

Though I walk through the val-ley of the shad-ow of death, I will fear no

e - vil: for you are with me, your rod and your staff com - fort me.

Congregation

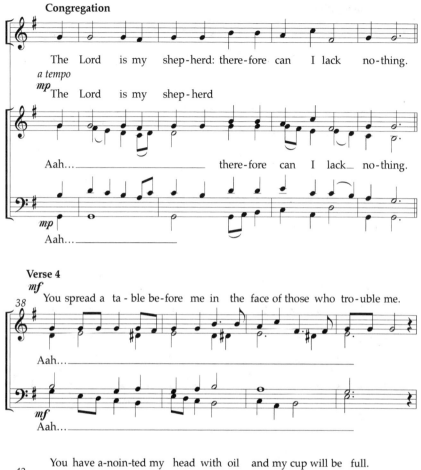

The Lord is my shep-herd: there-fore can I lack no-thing.

a tempo
mp The Lord is my shep-herd

Aah... there-fore can I lack no-thing.

mp
Aah...

Verse 4

mf
You spread a ta-ble be-fore me in the face of those who tro-uble me.

38

Aah...

mf
Aah...

You have a-noin-ted my head with oil and my cup will be full.

42

Aah...

Aah...

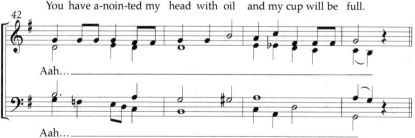

Congregation

The Lord is my shep-herd: there-fore can I lack no-thing.

The Lord is my shep-herd:

Aah... there-fore can I lack no-thing.

Aah...

Verse 5

Aah... Aah...

Aah... Aah...

Sure-ly your good-ness and lov-ing kind-ness will fol-low me all the

Aah...

days of my life; And I shall dwell in the house of the Lord for-ev-er.

rit.

98

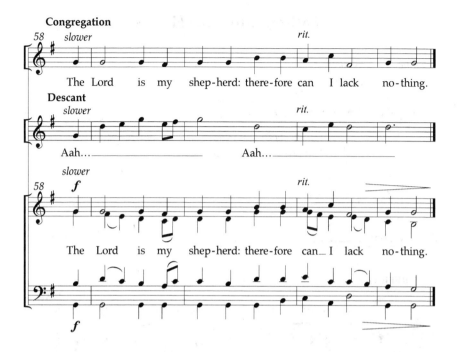

Congregation

slower *rit.*

The Lord is my shep-herd: there-fore can I lack no-thing.

Descant

slower *rit.*

Aah... Aah...

slower *f* *rit.*

The Lord is my shep-herd: there-fore can I lack no-thing.

f

Father, Into Your Hands

In - to your hands I com - mend my__ spi -
De - li - ver__ me from the hands of

rit. It is you who will re - deem me, Lord.
those who__ hate__ me.

To Refrain

VERSE 2

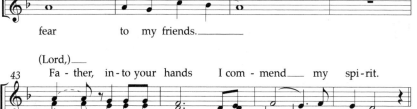

2. In the face of all my foes I__ am a re - proach, an__

ob - ject of scorn__ to my neigh - bours, and of

fear to my friends.__

(Lord,)__
Fa - ther, in - to your hands I com - mend__ my spi - rit.

(Lord,)__
Fa - ther, in - to your hands__ I com - mend my spi - rit.

Fa - ther, Fa - ther, Fa - ther, Fa - ther.
(Lord,__ Lord,__ Lord,__ Lord.)__

VERSE 3

3. Those who see me__ in the street run__ far a-way from me.

I am like a dead__ man, for-got-ten in men's hearts,

like a thing____ thrown a-way.

To Refrain

VERSE 5

5. Let your face shine__ on__ your ser-vant, save me in your love.

Be strong, let your heart__ take cour-age, all who hope in the

Lord, all who hope__ in the Lord.

(Lord,)____
Fa - ther, in - to your hands I com-mend__ my spi-rit.

(Lord,)____
Fa - ther, in - to your hands I com-mend my spi-rit.

Fa - ther, Fa - ther, Fa - ther, Fa - ther.
(Lord,____ Lord,__ Lord,__ Lord.)____

Like The Deer That Yearns For Running Streams

Psalm 42   *Noel Henry*

Responsorial Psalm For The Ascension

Psalm 46:2-3, 6-9; R/. v.6   *Michael Weedle*

Refrain

God goes up with shouts of joy, the

Lord goes up with trum - pet blast.

To Verses
Last Time Fine

Verses

1. All peoples clap your hands,
2. God goes up with shouts of joy, the
3. God is king of all the earth, sing

cry to God with shouts of joy, for the
Lord goes up with trum - pet blast,
praise with all your skill.

Lord the most high we must fear,
sing praise for God, sing praise,
God is king o - ver the nations,

To Refrain

great king over all the earth.
sing praise to our king, sing praise.
God reigns on his ho - ly throne.

In The Shadow of Your Wings, Lord

Based on Psalm 63

Ephrem Feeley

des - ert seeks wa - ter, my soul thirsts for you. Let me

see_you in the sanc-tua-ry, to see your might and glo-ry.

In the shad-ow of your wings, Lord, I sing, I sing for

joy; for your hand keeps me safe, Lord, my

joy; for your hand keeps me safe, Lord, my

soul clings— to you.—

52 Cantor

For your con - stant love is bet-ter than life, than life it -

Oo... Oo...

56

self, and so I will praise you, and thank you all my

Oo... Oo...

60

life. I will lift my hands in pray'r to you, a

Oo...

63

ban - quet for my soul.

Oo...

Choir + Assembly (m. 67)

In the shad-ow of your wings, Lord, I sing, I sing for joy; for your hand keeps me safe, Lord, my

joy; for your hand keeps me safe, Lord, my

soul clings to you.

Cantor (m. 78)

As I lie in bed, I re-mem-ber you, all night long I think of you; for you have been my help, Lord, and so I sing for joy!

Descant

In your shad - ow

Assembly

In the shad-ow of your wings, Lord, I

I sing for joy; for your hand keeps me safe,— Lord, my

sing, I sing for joy; for your hand keeps me safe, Lord, my

soul clings to you.

soul clings to you.

Canfaidh Mé De Shíor

Salm 88

Michael Weedle

Freagra

Voice

Can-faidh mé de shíor faoi do bhuan-ghrá___ a Thiar-na.

Véarsaí

1. Fuair mé Dái - ví mo ghiolla:
2. Beidh mo dhílseacht leis is mo bhuan - [-] ghrá;

rinne mé é a ungadh le m'o - la naofa
agus i m'ainmse is ea a ard - ófar a neart.

ionas go mbeadh mo lámh leis de shíor,
Déarfaidh sé liom: "Is tú___ m'athair,

is go neart - ódh mo chuisle é.
is tú mo Dhia agus car - raig mo shlánaithe."

'S Ón Tiarna Féin 'Tá Mo Chúnamh

Salm 121

Sr. Colmcille Ní Chonáin
arr. Philip Carty

Tiar - na féin 'tá mo chún - amh, a rin - ne___ neamh a - gus

tal - amh. 'S' an Tiar - na do ghar - da is do dhí - dean

a - gus___ é ar do dheis de shíor; Ní bhuail - fidh an ghrian thú i

rith an___ lae ná an ré i lár na h–oich - e. 'S ón

Tiar - na féin 'tá mo chún - amh. a rin - ne___ neamh a - gus

tal - amh. 'S ón Tiar - na féin 'tá mo chún - amh, a

rin - ne___ neamh a - gus tal - amh. Coim - eád - faidh an Tiar - na thú ón

ui - le___ olc, coim - eád - faidh sé d'an - am slán. Coim-

eád - faidh an Tiar - na thú ag___ im - eacht is ag teacht, a - nois, a - nois is

Cantor f

Ón Tiar - na féin___ ón Tiar - na féin___

All
(except Cantor)
f

choí - che. 'S ón Tiar - na féin 'tá mo chún - amh, a

neamh a - gus tal - lamh. Tiar - na___ féin___ 'tá mo

rin - ne___ neamh a - gus tal - amh. 'S ón Tiar - na féin 'tá mo

chún - amh, a rin - ne___ neamh a - gus tal - amh.

chún - amh, a rin - ne___ neamh a - gus tal - amh.

From The Lord Alone Comes My Help

Psalm 121 - ICEL Psalter
adapted by PK

Sr. Colmcille Ní Chonáin
arr. Philip Carty

vaa - tion, the Lord the___ mak - er of heav'n and earth.

Cantor

May God, ev - er___ wake - ful, keep___ you from___

stum - bling; the guard - ian of Is - ra - el

All

nei - ther rests nor sleeps, a pro - tect - or, at our side.___ From the

Lord___ a - lone comes my help, my___ strength, from God, Cre - a - tor of

heav'n and earth; the___ Lord is my help, my sal - va - tion, the

Cantor *mf*

Lord the___ mak - er of heav'n and earth. The sun shall not harm you by

day___ nor the___ moon at___ night. God

shel - ters you from e - vil, pro - tect - ing you life, keep - ing

watch both now and al - ways. From the Lord_____ a - lone comes my help, my_____ strength, from God, Cre - a - tor of heav'n and earth; the___ Lord is my help, my sal - va - tion, the Lord the_____ mak - er of heav'n and earth.

I Rejoiced When I Heard Them Say

Based on Psalm 122

Patrick Killeen

I re-joiced when I heard them say: 'Let us go to God's＿house!'

On our way we will praise＿his name. Let us go now＿to God's house.

1. I re - joiced when I   heard them   say:
2. Jerusalem is   built   as a   city,
3. Praising the Lord's name is   Israel's   Law;

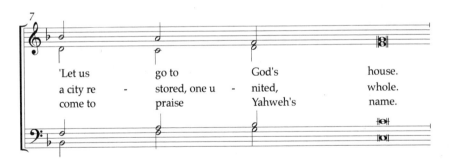

'Let us   go to   God's   house.
a city re - stored, one u - nited,   whole.
come to   praise   Yahweh's   name.

And | now our | feet are | standing
It is | here that the | tribes go | up,
There were | set the | thrones of | judgement

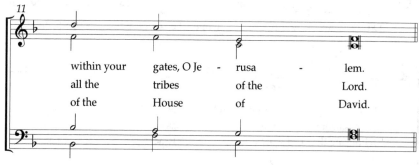

within your | gates, O Je - rusa - lem.
all the | tribes | of the | Lord.
of the | House | of | David.

What Marvels The Lord Worked for Us

Psalm 126

Cyril Murphy (arr. Stephen Dean)

Cantor: What mar-vels the Lord worked for us,— in-deed we were glad.

All: What mar-vels the Lord worked for us,— in-deed we were glad.

Verse 1
When the Lord de-liv-er'd Zi-on from bond-age it seem'd like a dream. Then was our mouth filled with laugh-ter, on our lips there were songs.

Congregation

What mar - vels the Lord worked__ for us,___
What mar - vels the Lord worked__ for us,___

What mar - vels the Lord worked__ for__ us,___

in - deed we were glad.
in - deed we were glad.

in - deed we were glad.

Verse 2

De -liv - er us, O__ Lord, from our bond-age as streams in dry

land. Those who are sow - ing in tears will sing__ when they

reap! **All** What mar - vels the Lord

Aah...

worked____ for us,____ in - deed we were glad.

They go out car - ry - ing seed for the sow - ing,

mm...____

full____ of tears. They come back carry - ing their

full of tears.____ They come back, aah...____

sheaves, full___ of___ song.

full of___ song.___

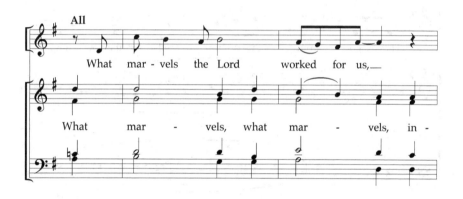

All

What mar - vels the Lord worked for us,___

What mar - vels, what mar - vels, in -

deed we were glad.

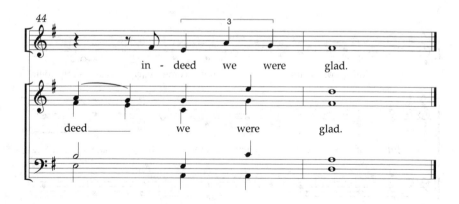

in - deed we were glad.

deed___ we were glad.

deed___ we were glad.

Alleluia, Give Thanks to God

Psalm 136

Yvonne Cairns
arr. Ciaran Tackney

Give thanks to the King of kings: HIS LOVE IS EV-ER-LAST-ING.
HIS LOVE IS EV-ER-LAST-ING.

ING. God of gods and Lord of lords: HIS
ING.
HIS

To Verses; Last Time Fine

LOVE IS EV - ER - LAST - ING.

To Verses; Last Time Fine

LOVE IS EV - ER - LAST - ING.

Verses

1. He spread out the earth up-on the wa -
2. He brought his ser-vant Is - ra - el out of E -
3. His love pro-vides for ev' - ry liv - ing crea -

124

ters._____ In wis - dom made___ the
gypt._____ Held___ back the waves___ and
ture._____ He re - mem - bered us___ and

heav - ens and great lights. The
led them through the sea. With
saved us from our foes. He

(1.) sun to gov - ern day_____ the moon and___

(2.) migh - ty hand___ and out - stretched arm___ God
(3.) res - cued and___ pro - tect - ed us___ to

stars to rule by night.___ His love en -
set his peo - ple free.___ His love en -
let all peo - ple know.___ His love en -

HIS LOVE EN -

D.S. al Fine

dures for ev - er.___

D.S. al Fine

DURES_____ FOR - EV - ER.___

125

I Will Bless Your Name For Ever

Psalm 144

Helen Walsh
piano arr. Andrew J. Mackriell

2. The Lord is kind and mer - ci - ful, com-

Ooh ___ Ooh ___

pas - sion - ate to all his crea - tures. How good is the

___ Ooh ___ Ooh ___

Lord ___ to all. Slow to an - ger, a-

___ Ooh ___ Ooh ___

bound - ing in love. I will bless your name for

___ I will bless your name for

ev - er, I will bless your name, O God, my King. ___

ev - er, I will bless your name, O God, my King. ___

3. The Lord is just in all his ways and lov - ing in

all___ his___ deeds._____ The Lord is near__ to
all who call up-on him, to all who call up-on him in truth.

I will bless your name for ev - er,
I__ will bless_____ your name for ev - er,

I will bless your name, O God, my King._____
I__ will bless your name, O God,__ my King._____

4. All_____ your crea-tures shall thank you O Lord,
Ooh_____ Ooh_____

and your friends shall re-peat___ your bless - ings._____ They shall
_____ Ooh_____

speak of the glo-ry of your___ reign and de-
Ooh_____ Ooh_____

clare your might, O God, my God.
Ooh_____

I will bless your name for ev - er,
I___ will bless___ your name for ev - er,

I will bless your name, O God, my King.___
I___ will bless your name, O God,__ my King.___

A Blessing: For Peace

Based on Matthew 5:8-10;   *Jan van Putten*

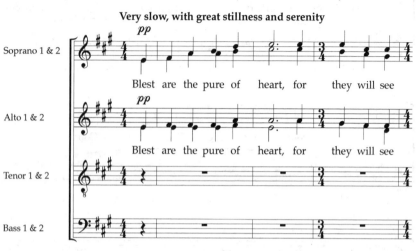

Alone With None But Thee, My God

*In glad memory of Dr. Joseph Groocock,
Teacher, Mentor and Friend of long ago*

*Attributed to
St. Columba*

Ruarc Gahan

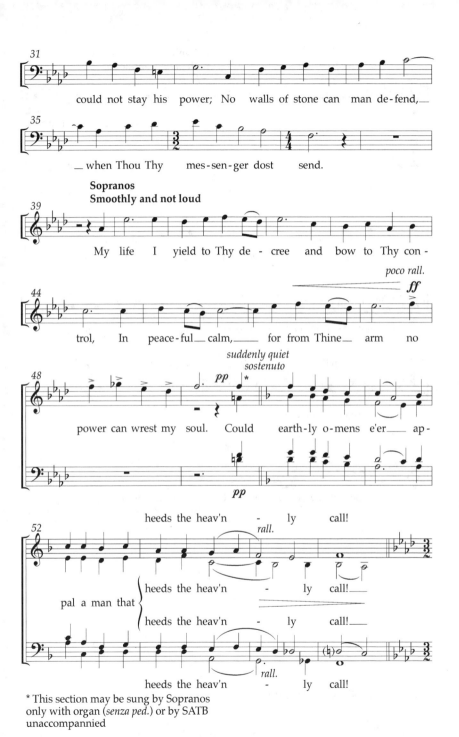

could not stay his power; No walls of stone can man de-fend,__ when Thou Thy mes-sen-ger dost send.

Sopranos
Smoothly and not loud

My life I yield to Thy de - cree and bow to Thy con -

poco rall.

ff

trol, In peace-ful__ calm,____ for from Thine__ arm no

suddenly quiet
sostenuto

pp

power can wrest my soul. Could earth-ly o-mens e'er____ ap-

pp

heeds the heav'n - ly call!

rall.

pal a man that heeds the heav'n - ly call!__

heeds the heav'n - ly call!__

heeds the heav'n - ly call!

rall.

* This section may be sung by Sopranos
only with organ (*senza ped.*) or by SATB
unaccompannied

133

The child of God can fear no ill, his cho-sen dread no foe; we leave our fate with Thee, and wait Thy bid-ding when to go. 'Tis not from chance our com-fort springs; Thou art our trust, O King of Kings. A-lone with none but thee my God, I jour-ney on my way.

* lower part optional for Altos & Basses

A Blessing of the Dead

Based on Revelation (Apocalypse) 14:13
(King James' version)

Jan van Putten

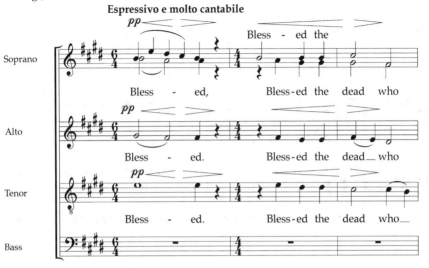

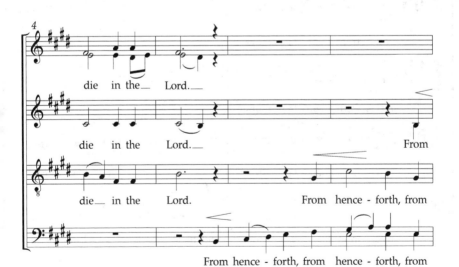

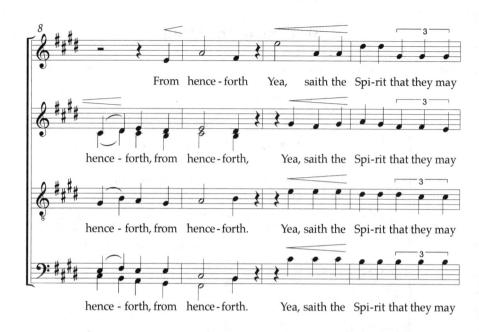

8

From hence-forth   Yea,   saith the Spi-rit that they may

hence - forth, from hence-forth,   Yea, saith the Spi-rit that they may

hence - forth, from hence-forth.   Yea, saith the Spi-rit that they may

hence - forth, from hence - forth.   Yea, saith the Spi-rit that they may

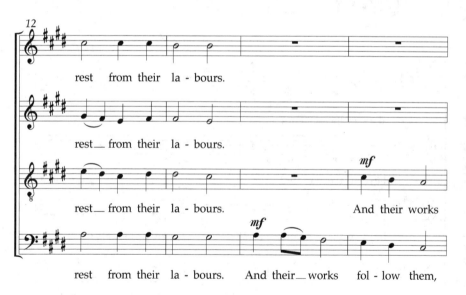

12

rest   from their   la - bours.

rest__ from their   la - bours.

rest__ from their   la - bours.   And their works

rest   from their   la - bours.   And their__ works   fol - low them,

più mosso

And their works fol -

And their works fol - low them, and their works fol - low them,

fol - low them, and their works fol - low them, and their works

and their works fol - low them, and their works fol - low them,

a tempo

low them, fol - low — them. Bless - ed.

and their works fol - low them. — Bless - ed.

fol - low them, fol - low them. Bless - ed.

and their works fol - low them.

A Gaelic Blessing

Bernard Sexton

140

A Choral Flourish

from Psalm 150

William McBride

breath, Let ev' - ry thing that has breath,

Let ev' - ry thing praise_____ praise_____ the Lord!

O How Amiable Are Thy Dwellings

Psalm 84

William McBride (arr. Michael Casey)

Blest are they that__ dwell in thy house, they will al-ways be prais-ing__ Thee. O how a-mia-ble__ are thy dwell-ings, Thou Lord__ of Hosts. Thou Lord__ of__ Hosts.

Lead Me, Lord

William McBride

148